Who's in Love
with Arthur

ISBN 979-11-86701-06-5 14740

Longtail Books

For the Krensky family: Steve, Joan,
Peter, and Andrew

Chapter 1

Outside Lakewood Elementary School, it was raining hard. But inside the **gym**, it was nice and dry, and the students were dancing to country music.* Square dancing* was a school **tradition** on rainy days.

Mrs. MacGrady, who ran the school **cafeteria**, was their caller.* She **led** them through the different steps.

★ country music 컨트리음악. 미국 남부 및 서부 지역에서 발달한 대중음악.

＊ square dance 스퀘어댄스. 미국의 대표적인 포크댄스로 네 쌍의 남녀가 마주 서서 정사각형을 이루며 추는 춤이다.

＊ caller 스퀘어댄스나 포크댄스에서 그 다음 스텝이나 동작을 외쳐서 알리는 사람.

"**Swing** your partner round and round," she said. "That's it! Keep swinging."

Arthur and Francine were managing their swing nicely, but not all the couples in their square★ were as good. As Binky swung Muffy around, her feet kept leaving the ground.

"Not so fast, Binky!" Muffy **complain**ed. "I'm not a helicopter."

Mrs. MacGrady **clap**ped her hands. "Side couples! Up to the middle, **high five**! And now **scoot** back!"

Binky **lumber**ed **forward**, **yank**ing Muffy along with him.

"**Look out**!" she cried as she was **hurl**ed off-**balance** into Francine.

"Hey!" said Francine. "**Watch it!**"

Muffy slowly **pick**ed **herself up**. "It's not my **fault**," she said. "Binky threw me!"

★ square 스퀘어댄스와 같은 춤에서 파트너끼리 서로 마주한 포지션을 말한다.

6

Arms swinging madly, Binky hoedowned* **backward** to his **spot**. His **elbow knock**ed the Brain to one side. The Brain **step**ped **on** Sue Ellen's foot. Sue Ellen **slip**ped and fell onto Francine. In another moment, they were all slipping, falling, and most of all, complaining.

Mrs. MacGrady shut off the boom box.* "I think that's enough for today," she said. "You were all very **light on your feet**." She **glance**d at Binky. "And I know the **rest** of you are trying your best."

Gym was the last class of the day. All the kids returned to Mr. Ratburn's classroom to **gather** their things before the bell rang.

"Did you say something?" Francine asked Muffy as she passed Muffy's desk.

"No," said Muffy.

★ **hoedown** 경쾌한 스퀘어댄스를 가리키는 단어로, 여기서는 동사로 쓰여 '경쾌하게 춤을 추다'라고 해석할 수 있다.
★ **boom box** 대형 라디오 카세트 플레이어.

After Mr. Ratburn **dismiss**ed them, Francine, Muffy, and Arthur **head**ed for the school **yard**.

"You're doing it again," said Francine.

"Doing what?" asked Muffy.

"**Mumbling.**" Francine **fold**ed her arms. "**Come on**, what's the **matter**?"

Muffy folded her arms, too. "Well, if you must know, I was just saying what a **crummy** day this was."

Arthur **nod**ded. "I don't like the rain, either."

"No, not that," said Muffy. "I'm talking about the dancing."

"Oh, that," said Francine, laughing. "You did **have your hands full**. But I think Binky's getting better."

Muffy **snort**ed. "Maybe so, but I don't know if I'll **survive** another hoedown like that." She suddenly **brighten**ed. "Hey, Arthur! Next time we have square dancing, will you be my partner?"

Arthur **shrug**ged. "Okay," he said.

"Wait a second!" said Francine, **frown**ing. "If you're dancing with Arthur, who's going to be my partner?"

At that moment Binky **burst** through the door behind them. His **shoelace**s were **untie**d, and as he came down the steps, he **trip**ped and **tumble**d to the ground.

Shaking his head, he **bounce**d up a moment later.

"I did that **on purpose**," he said. "Either that or the step moved."

Muffy smiled at Francine. "And you were **wonder**ing about a partner?"

"Oh, no," said Francine. "My health **insurance** isn't that good. I'm **stick**ing **with** Arthur."

Arthur looked from one friend to the other. "Don't I **get a say** in this?" he asked.

"No!" said Francine.

"But—," Muffy started to **argue**.

"Come on, Arthur," Francine **cut in**. "I'll give

you a **lift** home."

Francine **dragg**ed Arthur away to the street corner, where her father was waiting in his **garbage** truck. Arthur looked back once, but when he saw the **expression** on Muffy's face, he didn't look back again.

Chapter 2

Muffy sat down on a bench and **sigh**ed. The rain had stopped, and the sun was **peek**ing out from behind the clouds, but that didn't help. Her **mood** was still dark.

"Boy,★ do my feet hurt," she said.

"Maybe your shoes are too tight," said Binky, coming up behind her. He had re**tie**d his **sneaker**s, but one of the **knot**s was already coming loose again.

"These are very expensive shoes," Muffy

★ boy 소년이나 남자아이를 나타내는 명사가 아니라, 놀람이나 아픔을 나타내는 감탄사로 '어머나' 혹은 '맙소사'라는 의미이다.

explained. "They *envelop my feet in a cocoon of comfort*. It says so right on the box."

"Oh," said Binky, who never thought about enveloping his feet in anything but socks. "Your feet must be hurting for some other reason, then."

"Yes," Muffy agreed. "Some other reason— like a dancing partner who's always **step**ping **on** my **toe**s."

Binky **nod**ded. "Not very **considerate**. You should tell—hey, that couldn't be it. I mean, *I* was your dancing partner."

"I know."

Binky looked **confuse**d. "But I didn't feel a thing."

"I *know*," Muffy repeated.

"Huh," said Binky, **scratch**ing his head. "I guess I don't know my own **strength**."

Muffy sighed. "That's okay. I know you're doing the best you can."

"That's right," said Binky.

13

"But when Mrs. MacGrady says '**Swing** your partner,' she doesn't mean my feet should leave the floor."

"I **notice**d no one else was doing it my way. I just **figure**d their partners weren't strong enough."

Muffy stood up and began to **pace**. "It's not really your **fault**, Binky. The one I should be mad at is Francine."

Binky nodded. "She stepped on your toes, too, huh," he said **knowing**ly.

"No, no, she's a good dancer. It's just that she won't share Arthur with me. I mean, he's not her **personal property**. So why should she get to decide who he dances with? The way she acts, you'd think they were married or something."

"Married?" said Binky, **horrified**. "**No way!**"

Muffy **roll**ed **her eyes**. "Well, of course they're not *really* married. But Francine sure acts like she owns him. And she wasn't **afraid** to tell me to

keep my hands off!"

"Francine always **speaks her mind**," Binky agreed. "I never have to **wonder** what she's thinking, because she always lets me know. But she's good at sharing. So why won't she change partners with you?"

Muffy looked **sideways** at Binky. "Hmm, I wonder. Well, I'd better get going. I've got ballet class in an hour." She **glance**d down. "My feet are going to *love* that."

As Muffy **rode** off on her bike, Binky stood for a moment, thinking.

Suddenly his eyes grew wide. There *could* be one reason Francine wouldn't want to share Arthur. It would also explain why they went off **arm in arm**.

"Wow! I guess Arthur and Francine must be in love." Binky **shudder**ed. "I think I'm going to be sick."

Chapter

3

As Arthur **rode** his bike to school the next morning, he was still thinking about the day before. Something was going on between Muffy and Francine—that much was **certain**. However, it was something he didn't quite understand. Of course, there were times when it was safer not to understand these things. The problem was **figuring out** which times were which.

Binky was waiting for him at the bike **rack**.

"Hi, Binky," said Arthur.

"Good morning, Loverboy.* Where's your girlfriend?"

"My what?"

"Your girlfriend."

Arthur **fold**ed his arms. "What girlfriend?" he asked.

"I'll give you a little **hint**. Her **initial**s are F.F."

Arthur **blink**ed. He only knew one person with those initials. "You can't mean Francine?" he said.

"Of course that's who I mean. Don't you even know your own girlfriend's initials?"

Arthur put his hands on his **hip**s. "Francine is not my girlfriend! That's the most **ridiculous** thing I've ever heard."

"Oh, don't worry. Your little secret is safe with me."

"It's not a secret. THERE'S NOTHING TO HAVE A SECRET ABOUT!"

★ **Loverboy** 남자 친구 또는 멋쟁이 남자를 의미하는 속어.

Binky **wink**ed at him. "I get you, Arthur."

"No, you don't," said Arthur, shaking his head as he walked away. Sometimes, it was easier not to **argue** with Binky.

"ARTHUR AND FRANCINE SITTING IN A TREE," Binky **bellow**ed after him. "*K-S-N-I* . . . Wait a minute. Is that *K-S-I* . . . Oh, well. YOU KNOW WHAT I MEAN!"

Arthur didn't even turn around.

Arthur was still shaking his head when he got to his **locker**. He looked over at Francine, who was three lockers away. The thought of him and her, the two of them together, was ridiculous. **Absurd. Silly. Goofy. In fact**, when he stopped to really think about it, the idea was pretty funny.

"Hey, Francine!" he said. "Wait till you hear what Binky just told me. He thinks—"

Francine **reach**ed into her locker. "**Hold on**,

Arthur," she said. "I've got a surprise for you. Look!"

She **fish**ed **out** two cowboy hats.★ "I found them in our **basement**. My uncle in Texas sent them to us last year."

"Wow!" said Arthur. "They look real."

Francine nodded. "Yep. I'm sure they've seen a lot of time out on the **range**, **round**ing **up** the little **dogie**s."

"**Doggie**s?"

"No, dogies. That's **cattle**," Francine explained. "Don't ask me why. Anyway, I thought we could wear them the next time there's a square dance."

She **plunk**ed one on her own head and gave the other to Arthur.

"**Care** to dance, **pardner**?" she asked.

Arthur put the hat on and **tugg**ed at the **brim**. "Be right **proud**, ma'am."

★ cowboy hat 미국의 카우보이가 썼던 챙이 넓고 양 옆이 위로 말린 모자.

They laughed and did a little **twirl**. As Arthur **spun** around, he saw Binky at the end of the **hall**. He was **whisper**ing to the Brain. At first the Brain looked shocked. Then he started to laugh.

Suddenly Arthur stopped twirling.

"Whoa, pardner!" said Francine. "Give a gal★ a little **warn**ing next time."

"Sorry," said Arthur. "I was, um, getting a little **dizzy**."

"Okay. **By the way**, what was it you wanted to tell me? Something about Binky, I think."

"Oh, it's not important. I'll tell you later."

He gave the cowboy hat back to Francine and hurried into the classroom.

★ gal 소녀, 여자를 의미하는 단어 'girl'을 미국 남부 지방의 악센트로 말한 것이다.

Chapter 4

Later that afternoon, Francine and Muffy were changing clothes in the girls **locker** room. They were getting ready to play baseball.

"See you on the **field**," said Muffy.

"Hey, Muffy," said Francine. "I've got a new **glove** to **break in** today. Do you want to use my old one? It's the best!"

Muffy knew how much Francine liked her old glove, but that didn't mean *she* had to like it.

"I don't think so, Francine. It's used."

"Of course, it's used. That's what makes it so good! This glove has been in the middle of some pretty **amazing** plays. It **snag**s balls like a **magnet**."

Muffy **inspect**ed it. "Too bad my hand's so small. I don't think your glove will **fit properly**."

"Oh, well." Francine **shrug**ged. "Can you give it to Arthur, then? I still have to change my socks and **sneaker**s."

"Sure," said Muffy. She **weigh**ed the glove in her hand. "Maybe this will help him catch something."

Outside, Arthur was already in right field.★ Binky was standing near him in center field.★ He was making loud kissing noises with his lips.

Arthur turned toward him. "**Cut it out**, Binky. I'm telling you for the last time, nothing is going on between Francine and me."

★ **right field** 우익. 야구 경기장에서 타자의 오른쪽에 해당하는 외야 지역을 말한다.

★ **center field** 야구 경기장에서 외야의 한가운데 지역을 말한다.

"Yeah, right. You were holding her hand all during the dance yesterday."

"We didn't have much choice about that. **Besides**, you were holding Muffy's hand, too."

Binky stopped **smack**ing. "Hey, wait a minute," he started to say.

"Besides, if I felt the way you think I do, why would I **argue** with you?"

"So that I wouldn't know the truth," Binky said **triumphant**ly.

"Well, if I didn't want you to know the truth, why would I do things in **public** where you could see them?"

Binky was starting to get a **headache**. He had to **admit** that Arthur sounded pretty **convincing**. What he needed was more **evidence**.

"Oh, Arthur!" Muffy came running up to him. "I've brought you Francine's glove."

Arthur looked surprised. "Her special glove? The one she won the **championship** with?"

"That's right." Muffy handed it to him. "She really wants you to use it. Here. Try it on."

Arthur took the glove carefully. The inside of the pocket⋆ was dark where all the balls had hit it. There was a lot of **history** in this glove. He couldn't believe Francine would share it with him. Unless . . .

"Ooooooh, Arthur!" **coo**ed Binky. His **doubt**s had all been **swept away**. Francine would never have let *him* use her glove in a million years. But it seemed that Arthur was different. Special, even. Now Binky had all the **proof** he needed.

"Cut it out, Binky," Arthur **warn**ed.

"There's nothing to cut out, Arthur." He **point**ed to the **pitch**ing mound.⁎

Arthur followed his finger. Francine was

⋆ **pocket** 야구 글러브의 손바닥 가운데에서 집게손가락 아래까지에 해당하는 부분으로, 공을 잡기 위한 가장 깊고 확실한 부분을 말한다.

⁎ **mound** 마운드. 내야 가운데 부근에 불룩하게 솟아오른 부분으로 투수가 공을 던지는 장소이다.

standing there. She smiled and **wave**d at him.

"How does it fit?" she called out.

Arthur held up the glove and weakly waved back. "Fine," he said.

Francine laughed. "Only the very best for my **pardner!**"

Arthur's **stomach flip-flop**ped. Could Binky possibly be right? He knew he wasn't in love with Francine. But what if . . . No, Francine couldn't be in love with him.

Or could she?

Chapter

5

Arthur was sitting in a **booth** at the Sugar Bowl. He was drinking a milk shake and waiting for Francine to arrive. He took the paper from his **straw** and **tie**d it into a **knot**. Then he tried to untie it. The knot was being **stubborn**.

Arthur had made a decision. The best thing to do was to **get** everything **out into the open**. There was probably nothing to worry about. It was all in his **imagination**.

Arthur took a **sip** of his milk shake. Of course, it was easy enough to think all that. Believing it was another story.

When Francine came in, she hurried over and sat down in his booth.

"Hello, Mr. **Secretive**."

"Mr. Secretive?"

She **nod**ded. "Arthur, you told me to meet you here and not tell anyone. You said to make sure I wasn't followed and to **double back** on my **track**s. I feel like a spy."

"Okay, okay, so I want us to have a little **privacy**. That's not such a **big deal**."

Francine **snort**ed. "If it's not such a big deal, then why—? Oh, **never mind**. Anyway, I'm here. So, what's this big question that you wanted to ask *in private?*"

Arthur took a deep **breath**. He was pretty **satisfied** that no one was **eavesdrop**ping. He didn't want to be **overhear**d.

"Um, Francine . . ."

He pushed away his milk shake, trying to **collect** his thoughts.

"Hey, are you going to finish that?" she asked.

Arthur shook his head.

Francine **grab**bed a new straw and put it in Arthur's shake.

"Now, as I was saying . . . there's something we should probably **discuss**. Francine?"

Francine was **slurp**ing the milk shake.

"Could you stop slurping for a moment? I'm having a hard time thinking as it is."

Francine pushed the milk shake away. "Sorry. **Go on**."

Arthur **clasp**ed his hands on the table. "Sometimes two people know each other, or at least they think they do. But they really don't know each other as well as they think. I mean, one of them might know them both well, but the other might not. The other one might start getting some funny ideas." He looked at her **hopeful**ly. "Understand?"

Francine **rolled her eyes**. "You must be kidding.

31

I have no idea what you just said."

"All right. Let me put it a different way. **Suppose** there were these two, um, **dolphin**s. And they did a lot of **stuff** together. But they didn't think the same way about everything. And one day it happened that—"

A shadow fell on the **tabletop**. Arthur looked over Francine's shoulder and saw Binky and the Brain outside the window. They were **staring** at him and Francine. At least they were for a moment. When they saw Arthur looking at them, they **gaze**d at each other, **clutch**ed their hearts, and **bat**ted their eyes. Then they looked back at Arthur again.

"What about the dolphins, Arthur?" Francine asked **impatient**ly.

Arthur was still looking out the window. Now Binky and the Brain were **double**d **over**, laughing.

Suddenly Arthur stood up. "Oh, nothing!

Forget I ever said anything. Bye."

He threw some money on the table for the milk shake and **race**d out the back door.

Francine looked **puzzle**d. She finished the milk shake with a **frown** on her face. Boys could be very **strange** sometimes, and Arthur was no **except**ion.

Chapter
6

That night Arthur called Buster on the phone.

"I need some **advice**," he said.

"**Gee**, Arthur, you sound so serious."

"That's because I need serious advice."

"Okay. Let me get serious, too. I'll just put on my serious hat and **spin** the **propeller**."

Arthur told him what had happened. When he was finished, Buster was silent for a moment.

"You're kidding, right?" he said finally.

"No, no. I wish I was, but I'm not."

"Because," Buster **went on**, "it's really hard for me to tell if you're kidding over the phone.

I mean, I can't see your face. Your face always **give**s you **away**, Arthur. But since I can't—"

"BUSTER!" Arthur shouted. "Trust me. I'm not kidding. I'm very serious."

"**In that case**," said Buster, "it's just too . . ."

He started to laugh.

"You . . . Francine . . . I mean . . ."

"That's what I thought, too," said Arthur. "At least at first. It seemed like we were just good dancing partners. But that wasn't enough for her. She brought in **match**ing cowboy hats. And then she let me use her old baseball **glove**."

Buster stopped laughing. "That's true," he remembered. He had been at the game.

"I don't know what's coming next. Do you think I should be worried?"

"It's hard to know with girls," said Buster. "They can be very **mysterious**. Maybe you'd better keep away from her."

"How can I do that?" asked Arthur. "Francine

is one of my best friends."

"Yeah, but what if she tries to kiss you?"

Arthur **gulp**ed. "What?"

"That's what girls do when they like you."

"You're **making** that **up**."

"No, no, I heard some of the fifth **graders** talking one day at lunch."

Arthur **slump**ed down in his chair. His eyes were open in shock.

"Arthur!" Buster called out. "Are you okay? Arthur?"

Arthur **hung up** the phone in a **daze**. He went up to his room, lay down on his bed, and **stared** at the **ceiling**.

*Arthur was sitting on an **examination** table at the doctor's office. He was **shiver**ing, and his body was **cover**ed with a red **rash**. His mother and father were standing **nearby**. They looked worried.*

*"Mr. and Mrs. Read" said the doctor, "I'm **afraid** I have some bad news. Your son has*

cooties."

"Oh, no!" cried Mrs. Read. "My baby!"

She **rushed forward** to give Arthur a **hug**.

"Be careful," said the doctor. "He's highly **contagious**."

"But how could this happen?" asked Mrs. Read. "We try to make sure Arthur eats from all the food groups.★ And he **brush**es his teeth morning and night."

"It's not a question of **diet** or **personal grooming**," the doctor explained. "Arthur got the cooties from a kiss."

Mrs. Read **gasp**ed. "Arthur, is this true?"

"I don't know," said Arthur.

"Has anyone been kissing you **lately**?"

"Well, Grandma Thora . . ."

The doctor shook his head. "Family doesn't **count**."

Arthur stopped to think. "Well, then, only

★ **food group** 식품군. 일상적으로 이용하는 식품에 대해서, 영양성분과 유사한 식품을 몇개의 군으로 모아 분류한 것을 말한다.

Francine."

"And who is this Francine?" the doctor asked.

"A friend," said Arthur. "Just a friend. **Honest**."

"Is there no **cure**?" asked Mr. Read.

The doctor shook his head again. "We live in an age of **technological wonders**." He **sigh**ed. "But some things are still beyond the **reach** of **medical science**."

So this is what it's like to be **doom**ed, thought Arthur.

It was not a good feeling.

Chapter 7

The next morning Arthur got up slowly.

"**C'mon**, Arthur," said his father, passing by the bedroom door. "Let's get moving." He took a step back and **peer**ed at his son. "Are you feeling okay?"

Unfortunately, Arthur knew that dreaming about a **cootie** attack was not the same as being sick. "I'm fine," he said. "But I wish I didn't have to go to school today."

Mr. Read **nod**ded. "I used to have days like that. Especially in good weather." He **glance**d out the window. "But that's not a problem today.

It looks like rain."

Arthur **groan**ed. Rain. That meant more dancing.

When he finally **made it** down to the kitchen, everyone else was already having breakfast. Arthur sat down to eat, but he didn't feel very hungry.

"Mom!" said his sister D.W. "Arthur's playing with his food."

"I am not," said Arthur.

D.W. laughed. "Oh, really!" she said, **point**ing.

Arthur looked down at his **plate**. Without even thinking about it, he had **rearranged** his **scramble**d eggs★ into the shape of a heart.

"It's just your **imagination**," he said, **hastily** taking a few **bite**s.

"You do seem a little **distract**ed," said his mother, giving baby Kate her cereal.

"I have a lot on my mind," Arthur **admit**ted.

★ scrambled egg 스크램블드 에그. 계란에 버터나 우유를 섞어 프라이팬에 풀어 저으면서 볶은 달걀 요리.

"Like what?" asked D.W.

"Like what to do about **pesky** sisters who ask too many questions."

D.W. didn't care. "My teacher says it's good to be **curious** about things."

Arthur sighed. "Yeah, but sometimes you can find out things it would be better not to know."

When Arthur got to school, he saw Muffy, Buster, Sue Ellen, and the Brain. He didn't see Francine.

Maybe she's home sick, he said to himself. Not that he wanted her to really feel bad or anything. He just wasn't sure he wanted to **face** her in **gym** class.

He was just closing the door to his **locker** when someone **tap**ped him on the shoulder.

"Aaah!" Arthur shouted.

"**Bit jumpy** this morning, aren't you?" said Francine.

"Oh, it's you." Arthur backed up a step. "I thought maybe you were sick today."

"No, I just got a **ride**. I slept late. I had the **weird**est dreams last night."

"Me, too," said Arthur. Then he **brush**ed off his shoulder where Francine had touched him. He didn't know that much about cooties, but it was better not to **take** any **chance**s.

Francine **gave** him **a look**. "Are you all right?"

"Fine. Great. **Super**. Wonderful."

He started down the **hall**.

Francine followed him. "Is something wrong, Arthur? You've been acting a little **strange**."

He put his hand on the bathroom door.

"Wrong?" said Arthur. "Of course not! Why would you think something **silly** like that?"

"Well, let me see . . . You're jumpy. You're **nervous**. Oh, and there's the fact that you**'re about to** go into the girls' bathroom."

Arthur **jerk**ed his hand back from the door.

45

"Ah . . . I was just kidding. It was a **joke**."

"If you say so," said Francine. But as far as she was **concern**ed, the joke wasn't very funny.

Chapter
8

Even though Francine thought Arthur was acting **strange**, she still **saved** him **a seat** at lunch.

"Over here, Arthur!" she called out, **waving** to him across the **crowd**ed **cafeteria**.

Arthur **pretend**ed not to see her. He tried to sit at a table of fourth **grader**s. They **reluctant**ly **made room for** him.

"Thanks," said Arthur. "So, you guys come here often?"

The fourth graders **ignore**d him.

"Did you hear something?" one of them asked.

"I think it was a bug," said another.

"I wish that bug would **buzz off**," said a third. "I don't like it being here."

"Hey!"

Arthur looked up. Francine was standing beside him.

"Why are you sitting over here?" she asked. "I was saving you a seat. Didn't you see me waving?"

"Oh, well, I guess I wasn't paying **attention**. Anyway, I thought I would meet some new friends today."

The fourth graders **snicker**ed.

Francine put her hands on her **hip**s. "Fine. See if I care. I'm going back to my lunch. I don't want it to get cold."

She turned **sharp**ly and left.

Arthur smiled at the **rest** of the table. "She's a friend. Not a girlfriend or anything like that. Just a friend who happens to be a girl. That **make**s **sense**, doesn't it?"

The fourth graders **stare**d at him.

When Francine returned to her table, Prunella could see something was wrong.

"What's the **matter**?" she asked.

Francine shook her head. "Arthur is what's the matter. He's acting really strange around me."

Prunella was interested. "Like how?"

"Whenever I try to talk with him, he makes **excuse**s to **get away. Except** yesterday, when he **insist**ed I meet him in **private** at the Sugar Bowl."

"Hmmm . . . " Prunella had an idea. "Tell me something. Do his **cheek**s get red at these times?"

Francine stopped to think. "Yeah, I guess they do."

"And does he **hesitate** a lot when he talks?"

Francine **nod**ded.

"Well, then," said Prunella, "I think I know what's going on."

"You do?"

"I hate to say this, Francine, but I think Arthur is in love with you."

Francine almost fell over. "WHAT! Arthur? With me? That's **ridiculous**."

Prunella **shrug**ged. "I'm sorry, but he's showing all the **sign**s."

Francine **made a face**. "That's the **gross**est thing I've ever heard."

"It's quite common, really. Usually it shows up in older boys. Arthur may just **be** a little **ahead of himself**."

"Why me, though? Am I so **irresistible**?"

Prunella **sigh**ed. "It's a **burden**, I know. And with that burden comes **responsibility**."

"What do you mean?"

"Well, you have to tell Arthur the truth— that you don't love him. But you also have to be careful. You don't want to **break his heart**."

"You're right," Francine agreed.

"That means finding a quiet, private moment to share your feelings. It's a **delicate** situation."

Francine looked across the cafeteria at Arthur. He was not looking back. He was just staring down at his **plate**.

The poor guy, she thought. I'll have to be very **gentle** with him.

Chapter 9

Arthur approached the **gym** in slow **motion**. His hands were **clammy**, and the **sweat** was **gather**ing on his **forehead**. He didn't need a **crystal ball** to **predict** that the next hour was going to be a **disaster**. He just knew.

As **expect**ed, Mrs. MacGrady was **preparing** to **lead** everyone again in dancing. The kids gathered at one end of the gym.

Arthur and Francine **nervous**ly **face**d each other.

"Well, here we are," said Arthur.

"Yes," Francine agreed. "Here we are, all right."

"I don't see the cowboy hats."

"No," said Francine. "I guess I left them behind. I could run back and get them—if you want."

"No, no," said Arthur. "Anyway, I've been thinking."

"Me, too," Francine added quickly.

"Have you been thinking about the same thing that I have?"

"I don't know. What were you thinking about?"

Arthur **hesitat**ed. "Well, what were *you* thinking about?"

"You first."

"Okay," said Arthur. "Maybe we shouldn't dance—"

"With each other," Francine finished for him.

Arthur looked **relieve**d. "Right!" he said.

"Okay," said Francine.

They looked around for other partners. Arthur **pair**ed off with Muffy, while Francine stood next to Binky.

"All right, cowboys and cowgirls," said Mrs. MacGrady. "Let's see how much you remember from our last hoedown."

She turned on the boom box.

"**Bow** to your corner,* and bow to your partner," she said.

Everyone bowed **smooth**ly, **except** Binky, who **bent** down a little too far and **knock**ed his head against Francine's.

"Ow! Binky!"

"Sorry."

"Look, Binky," said Francine, as they waited for Mrs. MacGrady's next call. "You have to be careful. I only have these two feet, you know. I can't go to the mall and buy **replace**ments."

Binky **grin**ned at her. "I **suppose** you'd rather be dancing with Arthur."

★ corner 원래는 모퉁이 또는 구석이라는 뜻이지만, 스퀘어댄스에서는 자신의 왼쪽에 있는 사람을 가리키는 말로 쓰인다.

"I would not! Now pay **attention**. Here comes the next move."

Mrs. MacGrady **clap**ped her hands. "Now, everybody promenade!★"

Binky and Francine walked **arm-in-arm** around the circle. As they passed Arthur and Muffy, Arthur turned his head to see how they were doing.

Binky smiled. "**Jealous**?" he asked.

"Arthur!" said Muffy. "We're **fall**ing **behind**. Pay attention!"

She **jerk**ed him **forward**.

Arthur looked straight ahead. He tried to **concentrate** on dancing with Muffy, but he found himself thinking about Francine. Muffy wasn't a bad dancer, but she didn't have Francine's **enthusiasm** for square dancing.

"Muffy," Arthur **whisper**ed. "Don't you feel

★ promenade 무도회나 춤을 시작할 때 춤추는 사람 전원이 행진하는 것을 말한다.

like **stomp**ing your feet and **yell**ing, 'Yee-ha'?★"

"Why would I do that?" Muffy whispered back. "Every dance has steps to follow. I'm being careful. I have to follow the right ones at the right time."

"Now **thread** the **needle**!✸" said Mrs. MacGrady.

The kids started to **form** two **rows**, hands held high to make a **tunnel**. As the pairs **jostle**d for position, Arthur suddenly found himself **face-to-face** and **hand-in-hand** with Francine.

"What are you doing here?" said Arthur. "Quit trying to dance with me."

"*Me* trying to dance with *you*? *You're* the one trying to dance with *me*!"

"Francine, do I have to **spell** it **out** for you?"

"Don't make me say it, Arthur!"

They both took a deep **breath**.

★ **Yee-ha** 즐거움이나 기쁨을 나타내는 감탄사로, 카우보이가 많이 사용한다.
✸ **thread the needle** 두 사람이 양 손을 들어 서로 맞잡아 아치를 만들고 그 아치 밑으로 다른 사람들이 빠져나가는 놀이.

"I'M NOT IN LOVE WITH YOU!" they said together.

Chapter

10

For a moment, both Arthur and Francine were stunned. They faced each other open-mouthed.

Francine was the first to find her voice.

"You mean, you don't have a crush on me?" she said.

Arthur's mouth snapped shut. "No way! I don't get crushes. But what about you?"

Francine frowned. "I don't get crushes, either."

"But don't you want to kiss me?"

"Are you kidding? I'd rather have head lice."

"Ewwww, gross," said Prunella, who was standing nearby.

Suddenly Arthur and Francine **realized** that the dance had ended and everyone was **staring** at them. This could have been **embarrass**ing. Actually, it was embarrassing. But suddenly both Arthur and Francine realized the whole thing was so **ridiculous** that they **burst** out laughing.

"But I thought—," Francine started to say.

"Well, I was **positive**—," Arthur **stammer**ed back.

"Okay," said Mrs. MacGrady. "Show's over. Everyone, **grab** a partner!"

The music started up again. Arthur turned to Francine. He made a little **bow**.

"May I have this dance?" he asked.

Francine **curtsied** back. "Yes, you may."

"What about us?" asked Muffy. Binky was standing beside her.

"Don't worry," said Francine, "you still have—"

"Each other," Arthur finished for her.

"All right, Binky," said Muffy, holding out her hands with a **sigh**. "Let's try it again."

As Arthur and Francine started **skip**ping around the circle, Francine **grin**ned.

"Whew, I'm glad that's over," she said.

"Me, too," said Arthur. "Let's never let a **silly** thing like love come between us again."

"You **said a mouthful, pardner**! If I don't hear the *L*-word★ again for at least a year, it will be too soon. Now, let's show the **rest** of these **folk**s how to step out and **raise** some **dust**."

And the two friends danced like crazy till the bell rang.

_____

★ **L-word** 정확한 단어를 말하기 부끄럽거나 정중하게 표현하려고 할 때 그 단어의 첫 번째 글자에 '-word'를 붙여 말한다. 여기서 'L-word'는 'love'를 나타낸다.